WHY SHOULD I WASH MY BODY?

+ and other questions about keeping clean

and healthy +

Louise Spilsbury

Heinemann Library
Chicago, Illinois

Designed by David Poole and Tokay Interactive Ltd
Illustrations by Kamae Design Ltd
Originated by Ambassador Litho Ltd
Printed in China by Wing King Tong

07 06 05 04 03
10 9 8 7 6 5 4 3 2 1

Library of Congress Cataloging-in-Publication Data
Spilsbury, Louise.
  Why should I wash my body? : and other questions about keeping clean and healthy / Louise Spilsbury.
      v. cm. -- (Body matters)
Includes bibliographical references and index.
Contents: Why should I wash? -- How are germs bad for me? -- How often should I wash? -- Why should I wear clean clothes? -- Why should I change my socks? -- Why shouldn't I bite my nails? -- Why should I blow my nose? -- Why should I wash my hands after going to the bathroom? -- Why should I clean my room?
  ISBN 1-4034-4684-9 (HC)
  1. Hygiene--Juvenile literature. [1. Hygiene. 2. Cleanliness.] I. Title. II. Series.
  RA780.S68 2003
  613'.4--dc21

                    2003004883

Acknowledgments
The author and publishers are grateful to the following for permission to reproduce copyright material:
p. 4 Corbis/Imagebank; pp. 5, 13, 14, 15, 16, 17, 18, 19, 21, 25, 27, 28 Tudor Photography; p. 6 Corbis/David Woods; p. 7 Corbis/Layne Kennedy; pp. 8, 9, 10, 12, 23, 24, 26 Science Photo Library; p. 11 Corbis/Ed Bock; p. 22 Corbis.

Cover photograph by Tudor Photography.

Every effort has been made to contact copyright holders of any material reproduced in this book. Any omissions will be rectified in subsequent printings if notice is given to the publisher.

Some words are shown in bold, **like this.** You can find out what they mean by looking in the glossary.

CONTENTS

WHY SHOULD I WASH MY BODY?

Cleaning your body may seem like just another chore, but did you know that washing your body is the single most important thing you can do to prevent catching **infections?** Some **germs** can make you ill, and washing them away is the best way to stop germs from spreading.

Where do germs come from?

Germs are living things so tiny that you can see them only through a microscope. There are germs everywhere around us—in soil, in water, in the air, on our pets, and in our food. We could not survive in a world without germs. Many germs are harmless or even useful. However, other germs cause infections, such as colds, flu, and diarrhea, if they get into your body.

There are germs in soil, and this is why gardeners usually wear gloves. If you touch your mouth with muddy fingers, you may pass germs into your body.

How do germs get inside me?

Your skin is like armor. It is made up of **cells** filled with a tough substance called **keratin.** This protective layer covers almost your whole body. Most germs cannot get through healthy skin—they can infect you only if they get in through an opening in your skin, such as your mouth or nose.

Imagine that a friend at school has a cold. She sneezes and does not cover her mouth. Germs fly onto the desk. When you touch the desk, some of the germs rub onto your fingers. At lunch, you put your fingers into your mouth when you eat some grapes. Some of the germs move from your fingers to the inside of your body. Now you might catch the cold.

Germs can get into your body through your mouth. You can kill many germs by brushing your teeth twice a day for two minutes at a time.

5

How does washing help?

Most **germs** spread through contact. They rub onto your fingers from doorknobs or food or mix with sweat and dirt on your body. Washing with warm, soapy water gets rid of most germs. Soap attaches to particles of dust, dirt, and germs, so when you rinse off the soap, these things get washed down the drain, too.

Pets, such as cats, seem to be clean animals because they are always cleaning themselves, but their saliva (spit) contains lots of germs. Always wash your hands after petting animals.

WHEN SHOULD I WASH MY HANDS?

You should wash your hands:
- before eating or preparing food
- before you treat a cut or wound
- after using the bathroom
- after touching or playing with pets or other animals
- after playing outside or gardening
- after coughing, sneezing, or blowing your nose
- after handling trash.

What if I cut myself?

Germs can also get into your body when there is a hole in your skin, such as a cut. Cuts bleed because there are blood vessels just below the surface of the skin. If germs get into cuts, they can travel around your body very quickly in your blood. If a cut bleeds, press a clean, soft cloth on it until the bleeding stops. Then wash the wound with clean, warm water. After drying the cut, you can rub antibacterial cream on it, which kills germs. Wash your hands first and apply cream with a swab to keep the wound clean.

If a wound was caused by an animal's claws or teeth or by something especially dirty, ask a doctor to look at it. **Bacteria** from these things can cause serious **infections.**

Cleaning wounds is important. Covering cuts helps keep them clean.

7

HOW ARE GERMS BAD FOR ME?

Germs are tiny living things that take in food, give off waste, grow, reproduce (make more living things like themselves), and die. When certain germs live inside people, they can cause illness. The four most common types of germs are **bacteria, viruses, fungi,** and **protozoa.**

Bacteria

Different kinds of bacteria live in different ways. Most bacteria are harmless and some are useful, such as those that live in your **intestines** and help you to process your food. Yogurt is healthy to eat because of the bacteria it contains. A small percentage of bacteria, however, can cause problems, such as sore throats, tonsillitis, tooth decay, ear **infections,** pneumonia, and tetanus.

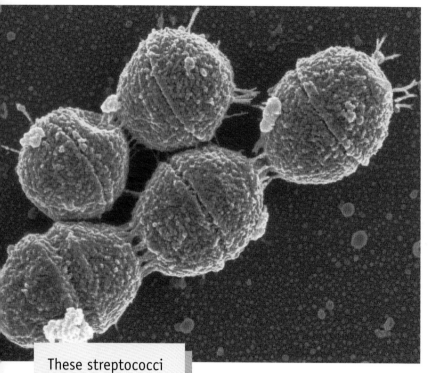

These streptococci bacteria, which cause sore throats, have been greatly magnified.

Viruses

Viruses are even smaller than bacteria. Almost all viruses cause disease. They spread quickly through your body. Diseases caused by viruses include chicken pox, flu, mumps, and measles.

Fungi

Some fungi have many **cells,** and others are tiny and have just one cell. Like other germs, fungi live on other living things, particularly in damp, warm places. Only about half of all fungi types cause disease in humans, such as athlete's foot. Penicillin is a helpful fungus that is used as an **antibiotic** to destroy bacteria.

Protozoa

Protozoa are germs with one cell that usually live in water. They are usually passed on in dirty water. Few kinds of protozoa cause disease in people. Some protozoa cause infections in the intestines, such as dysentery.

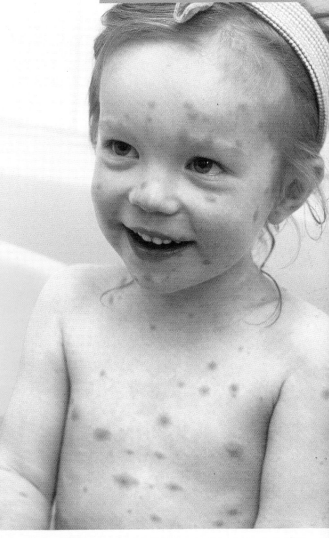

Chicken pox is an infectious disease that most people catch during childhood. It is caused by a virus.

How do germs hurt us?

Our bodies are made up of millions of tiny building blocks called **cells.** When **germs** get into your cells, they live there. They take in **nutrients** and **energy** from your cells, leaving them weaker. The germs also produce waste called toxins. These toxins are like poisons in your system and they make you ill.

This picture shows a white blood cell (colored blue) attacking **bacteria** (colored yellow) inside a person's blood. The cells have been greatly magnified so you can see this happening.

Does my body attack germs?

Your body has its own defenses against germs— the **immune system.** When germs invade your blood system, your blood quickly recognizes that chemicals in the germs, called antigens, are not part of your body. White blood cells in your blood make chemicals called **antibodies,** which attach themselves to the germs. This helps other white blood cells seek out the invaders and move in to destroy them.

How do medicines help?

If your body is unable to fight off the germs, you may need to see a doctor. Doctors can tell which germs have invaded your body by looking at samples of your blood. Then they match the medicine to the germ. Medicines are made of chemicals that attack the germs inside the cells.

IN THE PAST

In the past, before people understood that germs could pass on diseases, many people died from **infectious** diseases, such as cholera and typhoid. In England during the 1800s, a doctor named Joseph Lister encouraged other doctors to wash their hands regularly and to use clean equipment. Being clean greatly reduced the number of infections.

If you have to take medicine to cure an infection, make sure that you take exactly the amount prescribed by the doctor.

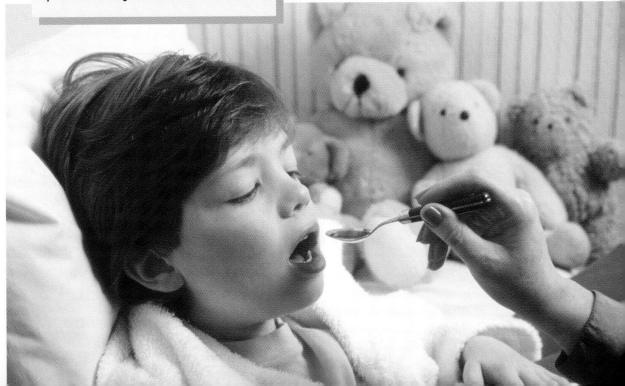

HOW OFTEN SHOULD I WASH MY BODY?

There are no simple rules about washing. How often you wash your body depends in part on how dirty you get. However, even if you do not look dirty, you need to wash off sweat, dead flakes of skin, and **germs** that you cannot see.

Shedding skin

Every day you shed millions of dead **cells** from your skin. Skin cells move up from the bottom of the epidermis (top layer of your skin), collecting tough **keratin** as they go. When they reach the surface, they die and form a protective outer layer. This process continues over and over again. When you rub your skin, some of the dead cells fall off and become part of the dust that you see on furniture or in the air.

This picture shows greatly magnified skin cells. Taking a shower or bath every day washes away dead skin cells.

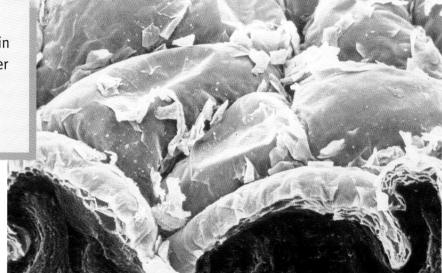

What is sweat?

When your body gets too hot, it sweats to cool itself down. You have sweat **glands**—body parts that make sweat—all over your body. They release sweat through the pores (tiny holes) in your skin. The sweat dries up from your skin, taking the warmth away and helping cool you down.

Sweat is made up mostly of water, but it also contains chemicals such as ammonia, salts, sugar, and urea (a form of waste left over when your body digests certain foods). Sweat itself does not smell. However, **bacteria** like to grow in warm, moist places. When they grow on sweaty skin, unpleasant-smelling chemicals are released.

Sweat glands are more common in some parts of the body, such as your armpits. That is why these parts get sweatier than others and why you need to wash them more often.

Why is my sweat starting to smell?

As you get older, you will notice that your sweat begins to smell more. This is because you are reaching puberty, the time of life when your body changes so that you can become an adult. Girls start puberty at any time between eight and fourteen years old, and boys start when they are between ten and seventeen years old. During puberty, your body starts to release a new substance from special sweat **glands** called apocrine glands, found mainly under your armpits. Although this substance does not smell, it mixes with **bacteria** on your skin and causes an odor.

Many people use deodorant on their armpits after washing to prevent body odor.

WHAT IS BODY ODOR?

Body odor is a mixture of smells, including:

- old sweat on which bacteria feed and then rot
- oils produced by your skin that collect and go stale
- dirt that gathers on your skin.

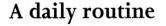

A daily routine

Although there are no rules about washing, it is best to get into good habits. Bacteria can build up on parts of the body with many sweat glands or where there are folds of skin, such as under the arms. In these places, dirt is easily trapped and hard to see. Taking a bath or shower every day or every other day is the easiest way to get rid of any bacteria. Use a clean, soapy washcloth to rub off dirt.

You can rub off healthy skin oils if you wash your face too much, however. Wash your face with soap or cleanser at night and rinse it with warm water in the morning to prevent the skin on your face from drying out.

Drying yourself is an important part of washing. Use a clean towel and make sure that you are dry all over, especially in folds of skin and between your toes.

WHY SHOULD I WEAR CLEAN CLOTHES?

It is especially important to change your underwear and undershirt every day. Because these clothes are worn next to your skin, they collect more dead skin **cells,** sweat, and bacteria than other clothes.

When natural body scents, dirt, and stale sweat gather on your skin for too long, they not only give you body odor, but they rub off onto your clothes and make them smell, too. The smell of dirty clothes can be even worse than the smell of unwashed bodies!

If you leave very dirty clothes lying around overnight, the **bacteria** on them can multiply by morning. If you wear these dirty clothes again, you can get an **infection** on your skin or inside your body (if you have a cut through which bacteria can enter). Dirt and **germs** on clothes next to skin can also cause pimples.

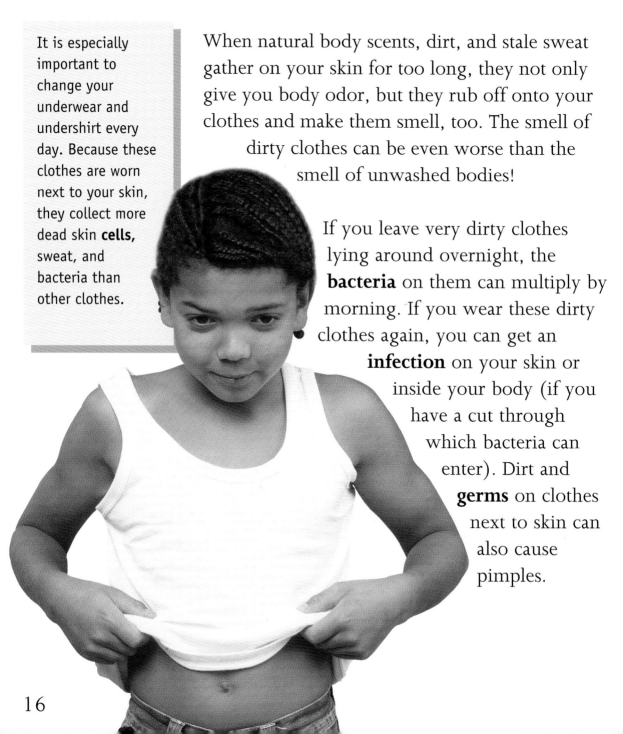

Healthy clothes

Some kinds of fabrics or styles of clothing are healthier than others. Nylon and some other human-made fabrics tend to make you sweat more. Cotton fabric allows air through and helps keep you cooler. On hot days, it is better to wear loose clothes, such as baggy T-shirts, which protect your skin from the sun but allow air to get to your skin to keep you cool. Tight clothes are more likely to collect sweat and become smelly more quickly.

Changing clothes for exercise helps keep you clean and healthy.

People change into special clothes when they exercise. They do this partly to be comfortable —T-shirts and leotards are made of stretchy fabric that is easy to move in, and shorts allow legs to move freely. People also change into workout clothes so that they do not make their ordinary clothes dirty and sweaty.

WHY SHOULD I CHANGE MY SOCKS?

Changing shoes after school allows your school shoes to dry out in the air, reducing the amount of bacteria in them.

You have more sweat **glands** in your feet than anywhere else on your body, and you spend a lot of time on your feet. When sweat soaks into your socks, **bacteria** soon multiply because they thrive in the warm, damp darkness inside your shoes. That is why it is important to put on fresh, clean socks every morning and preferably after exercising, too.

How else can I help my feet?

Keep your feet as clean and dry as possible. Wear cotton socks and different shoes every other day if you can. Keep your shoes clean by wiping off mud and dirt. If sneakers get stale and sweaty, they usually can be washed in the washing machine.

What is athlete's foot?

If you do not change your socks and keep your feet clean and dry, you can catch foot **infections.** Athlete's foot is a skin infection caused by a moldlike **fungus** that lives on the dead skin **cells** on your feet. It makes the skin between the toes itchy, red, flaky, and sore. Not only athletes get athlete's foot. It is usually passed on to other people in swimming pool changing rooms, where the fungus thrives on warm, wet floors.

You can treat athlete's foot with a fungicidal powder. But to avoid catching athlete's foot in the first place, wash your feet well and dry them carefully. Avoid sharing towels with other people because the infection can spread in this way, too.

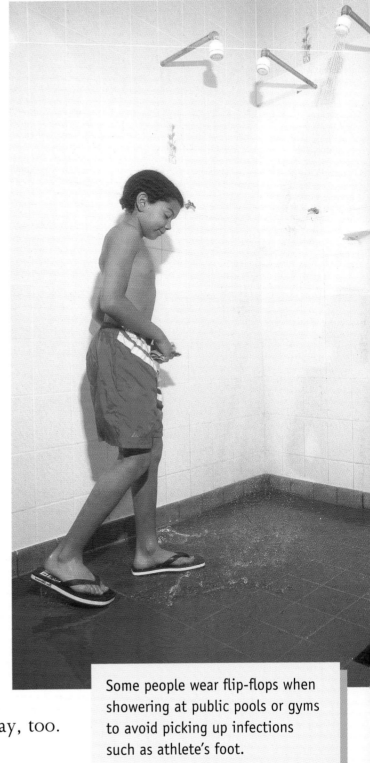

Some people wear flip-flops when showering at public pools or gyms to avoid picking up infections such as athlete's foot.

WHY SHOULDN'T I BITE MY NAILS?

Your fingernails have an important job to do. Along with helping you pick things up, they protect your fingertips. If you damage your nails, you leave your fingers open to **infection.** This is especially true for those people who bite their nails to the quick and even make their fingers bleed.

Dirt and **germs** collect under your fingernails. When you bite your fingernails, you put your fingers in your mouth and let these germs into your body. Also, biting your nails makes them more likely to break and become infected—and it looks unpleasant.

Trim your nails using curved nail clippers. When you cut, follow the curve of the nail but do not cut your nails too short.

How can I stop biting my nails?

The only way to stop biting your nails is to be very determined. To help you stop, you can buy a special clear nail polish that tastes bad. Some people give themselves a reward, such as a little present, for each week they keep from biting their nails.

Looking after nails

Fingernails and toenails need regular cleaning and trimming. When you wash your hands, clean out dirt that collects under your nails. Trim nails when they get too long, otherwise they can crack and break, and this can make them feel sore. Trim your toenails often so your shoes do not feel tight.

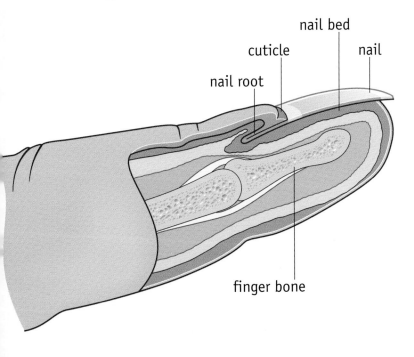

nail bed

cuticle

nail

nail root

finger bone

Cutting nails does not hurt because nails do not contain any nerves —just dead **cells** filled with a tough substance called **keratin.** The only part that is alive and growing is the root, just under the surface.

WHY SHOULD I BLOW MY NOSE?

Your nose is not just for smelling. It also contains hairs and a sticky liquid called mucus, which catches little pieces of dust and dirt that you breathe in to keep them from getting inside your body. Blowing your nose helps to get rid of these **germs.**

Because nose mucus contains germs and dirt or dust, you should blow it into a tissue to get rid of it.

Why does my nose run?

You always have a small amount of mucus in your nose. When you have a cold, your body makes extra mucus. Mucus soaks up the germs and contains an **antiseptic** that helps kill them. Mucus is usually clear, but when you have a cold, it becomes thick and green because of the **bacteria,** dirt, and dust in it. Your nose runs to get rid of the extra mucus.

Protecting the lungs

Your nose is the first line of defense for your lungs, the body parts for breathing. The mucus and hair in your nose catch particles to stop them from getting into your lungs, but bronchi (air tubes) in the lungs also contain some mucus to catch particles, too. If lungs become clogged with dirt or smoke, they do not work as well, and this can cause a range of problems with breathing.

WHY DO I SNEEZE?

If particles of dirt, dust, or bacteria irritate the lining in your nose, you sneeze to get rid of them. First, your brain makes you take a big breath (the "ah" part of "ah-choo!"). Then, your chest muscles squeeze your lungs, and air quickly rushes out of your nose.

If you do not cover your nose and mouth when you sneeze, you release germs into the air.

WHY SHOULD I WASH MY HANDS AFTER GOING TO THE BATHROOM?

It is especially important to wash your hands after going to the bathroom because **germs** found in **urine** and **feces** can cause many illnesses. If you do not wash traces (tiny amounts) of feces off your hands after you have wiped your behind, they can be passed on to other people and back to yourself.

Tiny pinworm eggs can get into the body from traces of feces. They hatch and live in the intestines. Your anus itches when the females lay eggs there. You can take medicine to get rid of them.

Germs

Germs passed on through traces of feces can cause diseases such as gastroenteritis and can spread pinworms, which can live in human **intestines.** If traces of urine are not washed away, they can pass on **infections.** People who have mumps can pass on the infection through traces of their urine.

Bathroom hygiene

It is also important to wipe your behind well after going to the bathroom. Girls should always wipe themselves from front to back. This stops **bacteria** from feces around the **anus** being passed to the urethra (where urine comes out). It is also important to clean your behind carefully every day when you take a bath or shower.

WASHING HANDS

It is important to wash your hands properly. You should:

- use soap and warm water from the faucet
- wash all parts of your hands —including wrists, palms, the back of your hands, between your fingers, and under your fingernails
- rub your hands together for at least fifteen seconds
- dry carefully with a paper towel, hot air dryer, or clean towel.

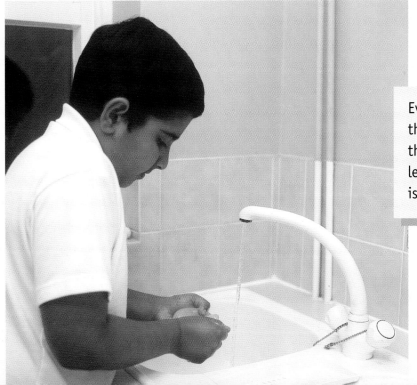

Everyone should wash their hands after going to the bathroom. It takes less than a minute but it is very important.

WHY SHOULD I CLEAN MY ROOM?

Keeping yourself clean and healthy means keeping your surroundings clean and healthy, too. If your bedroom gets dirty, **germs** will multiply and the number of tiny creatures that live in dust, such as dust mites, increases. It is normal and healthy to have some mites and bugs in your home, but you need to keep them under control by being clean.

This mean-looking dust mite is only 0.01 inch (0.3 millimeter) long! You are only able to see it because it has been magnified many times.

What are dust mites?

Dust mites live in the dust that builds up in our homes—in bedding, soft toys, and couches. They are so small that we cannot see them without a microscope. They feed on tiny bits of skin that we shed every day and that collect in dust.

Keep dust mites under control by dusting your room with a damp cloth and vacuuming often. Don't leave your clothes lying around or they will get dusty and dust mites will live on them.

A dust mite's droppings are so light and tiny that they float in the air when you plump up a cushion or run across a carpet. When people with **asthma** or allergies breathe them in, they can cause unpleasant reactions.

WHAT ARE ALLERGIES?

People have an allergy when their **immune system** reacts against something that is usually harmless to others. When the person comes into contact with an allergen (the thing they are allergic to), such as pet hair or dust, their immune system produces lots of **antibodies** to attack it. This releases chemicals called histamines, which make people feel unwell—causing red, itchy eyes and sore skin, sneezing, or even sickness and diarrhea.

Can my pet come in my room?

Some people are allergic to pet hair. Even if you do not have allergies, it is important to clean up pet hair because the dead skin **cells** and saliva (spit) on pet hair carry **germs.** You do not have to shut your pet out of your room—just keep your pet clean and free from fleas, wash any bedding that your pet lies on regularly, and clean your room often.

What are bed bugs?

Have you ever heard the saying, "Sleep tight, don't let the bedbugs bite"? Bedbugs are small insects that live in mattresses. They feed on tiny amounts of blood from people as they sleep. Their bites itch and may cause an allergic reaction. Keeping your room and bed clean helps keep out bugs and mites.

Keeping your room clean helps keep you healthy and makes your room a nice place to be!

AMAZING FACTS

- You grow a new top layer of skin every 50 days.

- Your skin is thickest on the palms and soles of your feet and thinnest on your lips and around your eyes.

- In 1 square inch (6.5 square centimeters) of skin, there are about 3 million cells and 100 sweat **glands.**

- Your saliva (spit) contains **antibodies** that destroy some of the germs that get into your mouth. We produce about 2 pints (1 liter) of saliva every day!

- Fingernails grow about 0.04 inch (1 millimeter) a week.

- When you sneeze, air comes out of your nose at about 100 miles (160 kilometers) an hour—that is as fast as an express train!

- Eighty-five percent of people who have **asthma** are allergic to dust mite droppings.

- An adult's feet can produce several tablespoons of sweat in a day.

GLOSSARY

antibiotic   substance that can kill bacteria

antibody   substance in the blood that protects the body by attacking germs

antiseptic   substance that destroys the germs that cause infection

anus   opening through which feces leaves the body

asthma   when the lining of breathing tubes are easily irritated and become narrow and blocked with mucus, making it hard to breathe

bacteria   tiny living things found everywhere. Some bacteria can cause disease.

cell   smallest building block of living things

energy   power that allows living things to do everything they need to live and grow

feces   solid waste produced by the body

fungus (more than one are called fungi)   living thing that can be made up of a single cell or many cells. Some fungi cause disease.

germ   tiny living thing that can cause disease

gland   part of the body that makes substances for use in the body or to be ejected from it

immune system   parts of the body that work together to defend it from disease

infection   kind of disease that can be caught by other people. This kind of disease is known as infectious.

intestines   hollow, coiled tubes near the stomach

keratin   hard protein that forms hair and the outer layer of skin

nutrient   chemical found in food that is good for the body

protozoan (more than one are called protozoa) single-celled germs that can cause disease in people and other animals

urine   liquid waste produced by the body

virus   tiny living thing that causes diseases in plants and animals

FURTHER READING

McGinty, Alice. *Good Hygiene*. Danbury, Conn.: Franklin Watts, 1999.

Royston, Angela. *Healthy Skin*. Chicago: Heinemann Library, 2003.

Silverstein, Alex. *Is That a Rash?* Danbury, Conn.: Scholastic Library, 2000.

INDEX